CW01664980

Seeing O
as Others See Us

Perceptions of the Church of England

Stephen Hance
National Lead for Evangelism and Witness,
Church of England

GROVE BOOKS LIMITED
RIDLEY HALL RD CAMBRIDGE CB3 9HU

Contents

Church Mission Society supports the Grove Mission and Evangelism Series
At Church Mission Society, we believe that every Christian is called to join in God's mission, whether that means crossing the street or crossing continents, and we want to set people free to put that call into action.

The cover image is copyright © Grove Books Ltd

Copyright © Stephen Hance 2021

First Impression August 2021
ISSN 2399-6536
ISBN 978 1 78827 185 1

Introduction

1

Background

A Christian presence in every community.

So says the strapline across the top of the Church of England's website, and it refers to something deep and distinctive in the history and ethos of the church. Most Christian churches see themselves as existing to serve, engage and reach their local communities. Archbishop William Temple's famous dictum, 'The church is the only organization that does not exist for itself, but for the benefit of those who live outside of it,' could be embraced by very many denominations and streams, not just Anglicans.

But the way that the Church of England lives out this aspiration is very specific. It happens primarily through the parish system, in which every street, house and individual is site d within a geographic parish. When a priest is appointed to a parish, they are entrusted with a share in the 'cure of souls,' responsibility for the spiritual life and well-being of everyone who lives within that specific parish, regardless of whether or not they are Anglicans, Christians of other denominations, atheists or adherents of other faiths. We express this in the way we offer marriage and funeral services to anyone who lives in the parish, Christian or not.

At the induction service when I became Vicar of Ascension Balham Hill in the Diocese of Southwark in 1999, a sense of that responsibility for all these people came upon me in a powerful and surprising way. This unique Church of England understanding is quite difficult to explain to those from other Christian traditions. 'What, you have a responsibility for all these people even if they never come to church, even if you don't know who they are, even if they don't believe in God?' Well, yes, actually.

However we understand, modify and apply all this, we might expect that the Church of England is particularly attuned to how it is perceived by all these non-attending parishioners, the people who live in all these communities that the church seeks to be a Christian presence in. After all, we do have feet on the ground in every community in the land, almost uniquely. And these perceptions matter. Not that we set out to make ourselves popular, or to make the gospel somehow more palatable, like a company conducting market research. Heaven knows (literally) that as a strategy this will be no more successful than it is faithful to what we have received. But these perceptions open doors of understanding to our mission field, highlighting challenges and opportunities for us. And while I think church people do care about these perceptions, we do not have much robust data to help us understand them. We can have lots of anecdotal evidence—something a friend said, something we saw on TV—but nothing more objective.

That is where this book comes in.

Perceptions of the Church of England

In 2020 the Church of England embarked on a process to articulate a new vision and strategy for the next ten years. The work was led by Stephen Cottrell, the Archbishop of York, and Dave Male, the Church of England's Director of Evangelism and Discipleship. As part of this process, background papers were commissioned from staff of the National Church Institutions. These papers were collated into a report on the strategic context in which our vision and strategy work was taking place, and made available to bishops, focus group attendees and others involved in shaping the work.

I was asked to prepare a paper on how the Church of England is perceived in our nation. My first degree was in sociology, and more recently I undertook some research on church health and community ministry for my doctoral studies, so I was delighted. I explain below how I undertook this work. The results were consistent, clear and to some extent unexpected. My aim here is to make this learning more widely available in the hope that it might shape the mission of the Church of England to engage constructively with the communities and individuals we exist to serve.

My sources were threefold. I undertook a review of recent media coverage of the Church of England. I reviewed all relevant research from the preceding five years or so, and I convened five round table discussions. The details of this research method are found in the Appendix, and the four key findings are discussed in the chapters that follow.

Key Finding 1: Benign Indifference 2

'Where Exactly is the Church?'

I was once vicar of a south London parish which had a very substantial building, hidden away down a residential street. Regularly I would receive a phone call from someone enquiring about a wedding or a baptism who would end the call by asking, 'And where exactly *is* the church?' Living nearby, they had no sense at all of where this building was, even if they walked past it from time to time.

Unfortunately, very many people in our society today have no particular sense or feeling about the church one way or the other. Those of us who spend our lives serving, leading, thinking about or wrestling with it tend to miss this. Most people do not think about us at all.

The most common perception of the Church of England is one of benign indifference. Cultural or nominal Anglicanism is collapsing, and many people see us as an institution in decline. Very many people have no real sense of who or what the church is, who it is for, or how it operates. This is especially true for younger people, but among older people too. The proportion feeling any connection with the church diminishes generationally. Younger Christians have a diminishing sense of denominational loyalty so that even those who are actively involved in a parish may join a church of another denomination in the future. This poses an existential threat to the Church of England.

The Mission Map of England

My colleague Canon Dave Male has produced a 'mission map,' dividing our population into six different groups according to their relationships with church and faith, as follows:

- Core Anglicans—200,000 (0.36% of the total);
- Regular Anglican worshippers—1.14 million (1.8%) of 6 million regular church attenders of all denominations (11%);
- Cultural fringe—10 million (18%);
- Indifferent—11 million (20%);

- Dismissive—23 million (42%);
- Other faiths—5 million (9%).

Those first two groups, the most engaged, are older than average and more female than male. Our cultural fringe—those who attend occasionally, towards whom a lot of our activity is focused—is the fastest-declining group. Thirty years ago, 18.4 million identified as Anglicans, according to the British Social Attitudes survey. Now it is 6.6 million. Meanwhile, the fast-growing group is the 'nones,' most of whom are dismissive of the church and disbelieve in God. These now make up the largest group in the population, and an even bigger percentage among younger people.

Hostile Indifference Among the Young

Levels of trust in the church remain generally high, but not universally so, and less high among younger people. For them, benign indifference can tip over into outright hostility on LGBTQ+ issues. The church's response to abuse scandals is seen by some as about the protection of the institution more than responding with justice to those who have been harmed. The experience of LGBTQ+ people is particularly mentioned by under-30s, and many who self-identify as such say that they have been hurt by the church. This hurt particularly relates to experiences where a local church promotes itself as being very welcoming to all, and only over time do the limits of that welcome to LGBTQ+ people emerge. For some the church has been experienced as hostile, unsafe, dishonest or insincere.

2020 was the year in which the Black Lives Matter movement came to the fore, and again the church's record in empowering Black people and combatting racial injustice is seen as less-than-stellar by many millennials. The lack of UKME people in senior positions of leadership in the church is highlighted, along with a reluctance to come to terms with the church's links with slavery and colonialism in an open and honest way, although the church is seeking to respond to these challenges.

So for some, indifference is more hostile than benign, born out of a sense of justice which is one of the evidences of the ways in which our culture has been shaped by a Christian heritage.

The National Church

There is particular ambivalence when it comes to the national role of the Church of England. Many are confused by the presence of bishops in the House of Lords and other manifestations of the church's establishment. Even some of those who are positively inclined towards the church do not understand this, and state that this feels archaic in twenty-first century Britain.

These findings create a concern that, as a piece of unpublished reasearch for the Church of England suggests, the church could almost disappear from view with few mobilizing to defend it, or even noticing it happening.

At a societal level, changes in habits (most notably following changes to the Sunday trading laws) mean that Sunday is no longer a day of rest. Instead, for many people, it is a day to run errands, spend time with family or, in many cases, to work. As a result, Sunday worship is not a priority. This applies even to those who have faith, who often do not feel that they need to go to church to have a relationship with God. This low priority of worship is coupled with a widespread view of the church as old fashioned and 'not for me' and, in some instances, negative experiences when people do attend church. This acts as a further barrier to attendance. Finally, those who do attend church often feel that they are judged for their faith. This means that they do not discuss their religion, which in turn exacerbates the lack of understanding of the church.

Implications for the Mission of the Church

The situation described above has implications for our mission. These include:

- *The people who we think of as our fringe are disappearing.* Decline in nominal Anglicanism will continue, with those who are not active members of a faith community increasingly identifying as 'nones.'
- *Many will believe church is not for 'PLU.'* When I was a Dean, a woman spoke to me as she left a carol service to say she did not realize that 'people like her' were allowed into the cathedral. With a committed core but smaller fringe, fewer people are likely to have had any positive experience of church, or to know people who have.
- *Younger generations are even less engaged with church, and those who are aware may be hostile.* Those who are Christians are more likely to be denominationally fluid, choosing a worshipping community for a season, rather than a denomination for life.
- *We have a new digital fringe to reach.* Our fringe is increasingly likely to be found online, made up of those who have found streamed worship a source of comfort or interest. This requires a significant

pivot on the church's part to develop good practice in serving, evangelizing and integrating online worshippers.

How can the church respond to these challenges and opportunities? Space prohibits a detailed discussion, but some areas for further work are clear.

- *Work harder at relationships and welcome.* If many people have no church experience or connection at all, positive or negative, we need to work that much harder to create relationships that can lead people into a journey of faith, being particularly aware of how one person's experience of welcome and inclusion, or otherwise, may shape the views of many others who have no experience of their own.
- *Consider how we address young people's spirituality—the 'spiritual not religious.'* Young people's lack of connection with or interest in the church is not indicative of a lack of interest in spirituality. Some suggest that the younger generations have a greater interest in spiritual things than their elders. The challenge is that they do not see the church as an ally in that quest. The church needs to consider how to respond to this. Online worship has been a good first step. We could offer more in the way of meditation and teaching on spiritual practices online as well as on-site.
- *Contribute to the common good.* The report from Theos 'Growing Good: Growth, Social Action and Discipleship in the Church of England,' demonstrated how important it was for a local church to be good news, not just to talk about good news.[1] This happens as churches roll up their sleeves and get involved with the felt needs of the local community, intentionally building a good reputation in a local community, which may create opportunities to share the good news of Jesus.
- *Partner not host.* In the COVID-19 pandemic there were anecdotes about local churches who were unwilling to get involved with local community action projects unless they could convene or lead them in some way. An assumed superiority lies behind such an attitude, which as we have seen is not justified. Churches can create opportunities to engage and build relationships by serving alongside others in the community from a position of humility, relinquishing any need to be in charge.
- *Clarity about stance of local churches on LGBTQ+.* The *Living in Love and Faith* process reminds us that this is a topic which the church

has struggled to find its way through. But whatever the outcome of that or other processes, we at least need to be aware of the impact our perceived discrimination against LGBTQ+ people has on our ability to engage with younger and more culturally liberal people. We will need to be willing to explain and defend whatever stance is adopted locally or nationally.

Looking ahead, our cultural fringe will most likely continue to decline, meaning that new relationships and positive perceptions beyond the church will have to be created and nurtured. The mission opportunities of online church will continue as well, and a new digital fringe is being created. An increasing proportion of the worshipping community is likely to gather online, either instead of or as well as offline gathering. The position of the church at the centre of the establishment will be under continued scrutiny, for example around the coronation of the next sovereign. The church will have to consider what case it wishes to make for this unique position in a multi-faith society. There will be an increasing interest in matters of faith and spirituality amongst the young. The church that seeks to engage them will have to speak of God, of the possibility of encounter with God, of the values of the kingdom of God.

3 Key Finding 2: Fondness and Appreciation

The Poor Old Church of England

In an article in the *Financial Times* from September 2017, journalist Jeremy Paxman writes:

> 'Oh, the poor old Church of England,' said a vicar friend when I told her I wanted to find out what made it tick. Her resigned tone suggested despair at any outsider 'getting' it. But on the whole, I admire the church. In many ways, the story of England is the story of her church, and there is something endearing about its endless anxieties.'[2]

In a round table discussion one participant described the church as being like an elderly maiden aunt. 'You don't go to visit her very regularly, and when you do you don't look forward to it, but when you get there it's really nice, and you wonder why you don't go more often.'

Television dramas tend to portray the Church of England in a fairly consistent way. Congregations are small, largely elderly, with more than their fair share of eccentric people. Clergy are well-meaning, kind, bemused and confused. Church buildings are historic and huge, and decaying through neglect. The church is an institution out of time, a remnant of an earlier and easier era, close to extinction. Yet there is something about it—a residual selflessness, a flicker of unfashionable values which might still mean something, a legacy buried deep in the culture of England—which continues to appeal. You might not want to be involved yourself. But you will be sorry when it is gone.

The second finding of my research is that, among those who do have a view, that view is largely positive.

Fondness Among Non-Anglicans

The view tends to be more positive among those who do *not* count themselves as Church of England members than among those who do. In one round table discussion a participant who described himself as an atheist listened to the comments of those who were committed Anglicans, and then commented that he seemed to have a much more favourable view of the church than them!

This warm feeling towards the church is described in quite specific ways as a fondness, or affection. People talk about 'the good old Church of England.'

Some of this is a kind of *nostalgia*. Former Prime Minister John Major famously said, 'Fifty years on from now, Britain will still be the country of long shadows on county [cricket] grounds, warm beer, invincible green suburbs, dog lovers, and—as George Orwell said—old maids bicycling to Holy Communion through the morning mist.'[3]

For many who are not believers, it is the *unthreatening* nature of Anglicanism that appeals. The faith of the Church of England, expressed in adherence to slightly arcane rituals, the maintenance of historic buildings with minimal resources, the willingness to engage with anyone and everyone, and a notable reluctance to say anything very dogmatic (or sometimes anything at all) about God, is all much more appealing than other more assertive varieties of religious practice on offer in the world today.

The church is seen as offering stability and continuity in a world in flux

But there is more going on here. The church is seen by many people as a *force for unity*, an institution for the non-believer as much as for the believer, an umbrella which offers stability and continuity in a world in flux. We live in an increasingly fragmented and divided society. The Brexit referendum and its aftermath were often cited in evidence, as was the increasingly embittered nature of some of our political discourse. Many express the view that as a society we need to find a way of recovering some sense of belonging and mutuality, but they do not believe there are many institutions capable of contributing to this. The Church of England is singled out as perhaps the paramount institution that might be able to.

At both a national and local level, the greatest level of appreciation is expressed for the church's engagement in *social action*. Food banks, toddlers' groups and homeless shelters are frequently highlighted. It is recognized that many of the volunteers, and indeed the key workers, on whom society depends are disproportionately Christians whose faith is often a key motivating factor in their altruistic actions.

There is much appreciation for the church's *buildings* and its role in securing parts of our national heritage. The church is responsible for a huge swathe of historic buildings, and cares for these with limited resources and little or no help from the state (contrary to what many may believe). Non-Christians speak as positively as Christians about visiting great churches and cathedrals, and may indeed have experiences of the numinous there, even if they do not use Christian language to describe those experiences.

Finally, and perhaps surprisingly, alongside people's appreciation of our heritage, there is also positive comment about *adaptability* and willingness to change. The massive move to worship online is singled out as evidence that the church can change rapidly when it wants to. It may be that in some people's minds the bar has been set so low that even a somewhat belated pivot to the online world is seen as an achievement, in the same way that some of us have been amazed how our less tech-savvy relatives have managed to navigate Zoom during the pandemic. But the perception remains.

Implications for the Mission of the Church

These findings highlight some challenges and opportunities. Six are highlighted here:

More Goodwill Than We Think

Among those who have a view of the Church of England, admittedly a minority, that view is more positive than negative. This should build our confidence to engage with those who do not presently identify as Christians. People may snigger at some of the perceived eccentricities of the Church of England (and don't we all?!) but a lot of it is kindly meant. This means that we do not need to be too anxious or apologetic when we ask others to partner with us, or to support us, or when we seek to talk about God.

Social Action Gives Authority

The most positive feedback that the Church of England receives is for our social action work. People know that we support food banks, street pastors, toddlers' groups and so on, and they appreciate it. The recent *Growing Good* report from Theos looks closely at the relationship between social action, discipleship and evangelism, and argues for their integration.[4] The report states, 'Churches should be encouraged to see their social action projects as primary sites of invitation and be expectant of the relationships that can grow through it.' Our social action gives opportunities to create other places of engagement, including for sharing the faith. We do not engage in social action *because* it gives authority or authenticity to our message and our faith. But nevertheless, it does.

Online is Cutting Through

The move to offering worship online through the COVID-19 pandemic has made an impression on those who have *not* personally participated, as well as those who have. Research for TearFund by Savanta/ComRes in the first lockdown showed that 24% had accessed worship online, and higher among younger age groups.[5] Some who were not previously part of our worshipping communities have found online worship helpful because of its accessibility, its anonymity, the security of being in one's own home, the flexibility to watch at the most convenient time, and so on. It is imperative that this continues to be developed and prioritized when the pandemic is over.

Public Theology and the Common Good

There is a gap between people's hopes of what a post-pandemic society could look like, and their fears of what may materialize. The church is one of the few institutions well-positioned to help bridge that gap. This calls for public theology, articulating the Christian values that could underpin the better society that we hope for and so helping to shape the common good. This is a role primarily for the national church and some of our episcopal leadership. Recent books by the Archbishop of Canterbury, *Reimagining Britain,* and the Archbishop of York, *Dear England,* serve as examples of this, albeit that more needs to be done to get those contributions into the wider public discourse.[6]

Appreciation of Our Strengths

Those who see the Church of England as their home are famously critical of it. In the same way that I know all the annoying quirks in my house that others might not see, active Anglicans are often better at explaining what is wrong with the church than what is right with it. (Exhibit A: Anglican Twitter!) Without losing the ability to be reflective and self-critical, we could get better at appreciating our strengths. This is not about curtailing comment or criticism, but of reminding ourselves of what we value about the church, and trying to make our criticisms less public, following the recent Church of England Digital Charter. After all, as Joni Mitchell sang, 'Don't it always seem to go, that you don't know what you've got till it's gone?'[7]

Missional Potential of Buildings

Our buildings are hugely appreciated, and how even those with no faith may have spiritual moments when they visit them. Some have always believed that 'the church is not the building' and of course that is true. But as a Residentiary Canon and then a Dean I realized how powerful an open, peaceful and prayerful building could be, enabling people to sit, to think, light a candle and pray. Not every church building is aesthetically beautiful, of course. But even an ugly 1960s church hall can house 'sacred space' with prayer stations, flowers, craft tables or whatever is appropriate. In many communities where church buildings are closed most of the time, there could be opportunities to make them genuinely multi-purpose spaces, serving the common good and bringing people over the threshold at the same time.

4 Key Finding 3: Local Trumps National

Where (and Who) is the Church?

As someone who works for the National Church Institutions, it is quite easy for me to default to picturing those institutions and the people in them when I hear the word 'church.' For many people, if they think about the Church of England, they do indeed think about bishops and archbishops, abbeys and cathedrals (although probably not Church House Westminster!). But for most, this is not the *first* thing that comes to mind. And how they feel about that *national* presence is largely shaped by how they feel about the *local* experience of church that they or their friends and family have had. Simply, for most people, the local trumps the national manifestation of the Church of England.

The Lens of the Local

A friend became vicar of a parish in an outer-London suburb. The church was well set up to be effective in outreach to the local area. It had strong links with the nearby school, a prime location by a busy thoroughfare and even had a car park! (Not to be sneezed at in London.) And yet local people did not think well of it, and did not choose to mark key life moments there if they had other options. A previous long-serving vicar had developed a reputation for being grumpy and difficult. He would mock or dismiss people's choices of music for weddings or funerals if he thought they were not suitable. He would get cross with children from the school. Many local people had tales to tell of bruising encounters with him, and many more had heard those tales. As a result, in that community, even though that vicar had gone, the church was seen as unfriendly, unwelcoming, not for 'people like us.'

My research demonstrated that positive or negative encounters, experienced personally or heard about, shape how people think of the whole church. Many of these encounters are around life events. A friendly, welcoming vicar, a priest who goes the extra mile for a funeral family, a parish church that is thoroughly involved in their local school, a church that serves vulnerable people, all make a positive impression. A lack of welcome or inclusion, a feeling that visitors are not wanted by a cliquey in-crowd, does the opposite. Fortunately, the majority of reported local encounters are positive, although not all. In an institution where there is so much diversity of approach and quality, this is a challenge.

What About the National Church?

Generally, comments about the national church and its leadership are positive. Archbishop Justin Welby is well-liked, and his contributions to our national discourse through his media appearances are rated highly. He is seen as down-to-earth, approachable, with wisdom forged in the crucible of his own experience. Although critical articles in the press may cut through from time to time, these are not representative of how the senior leadership of the church is perceived by many round table participants. One nationally-known broadcaster said in a round-table discussion, 'In Archbishop Justin you have the best figurehead you could hope for, but you don't make enough of him.'

What about the bishops' voices? On the one hand, I found that some people (although by no means all) are appreciative of the way in which bishops and other church figures speak out on issues of social concern. Poverty, inequality and racism are all seen as examples of issues where it is appropriate for the church to be engaged. One hopes that most Christians would agree that these are theological issues on which the church must reflect and contribute.

However, some feel that the issues on which the church engages, and particularly those on which the bishops speak, betray a left-leaning perspective, and the assumption of a consensus around that perspective, which does not exist—inside the church or outside it. Several people criticized the bishops' comments on the Dominic Cummings affair, not because they necessarily disagreed, but because they felt Cummings was an easy target for a kind of leftish self-righteousness. If historically the Church of England has been 'the Tory Party at prayer,' its senior leadership is now perceived by some to sit comfortably and consistently within the pro-European soft left and reluctant to challenge its shibboleths. The leadership of the church can seem quite detached from the political centre of gravity in a nation which has elected a Conservative-led government in eight of the last eleven general elections. Some feel that bishops and the church are out of touch with ordinary people. Some feel that the church contributes on issues which are relatively easy to speak about, without the confidence to engage in thornier matters. Someone said, 'The church hasn't found its voice yet.'

Has Anyone Seen My Diocese?

Sometimes the things people choose *not* to talk about can be as interesting as the things they do. A very striking finding of my research is how little impression the diocese makes on most people.

Perhaps this is not surprising. After all, while we might expect reasonably aware non-church people to have seen enough of the Archbishop of Canterbury to have an opinion about him, this is not necessarily true in the same way for the diocesan bishop. Perhaps people who read the local media assiduously might have some sense of who the bishop is, or what goes on in the cathedral, but other less conscientious observers of the local scene may not.

But we might anticipate that people would be as aware of the bishop as the vicar, as conscious of the cathedral as the parish. Yet my research suggests this is not the case. While many people shared their perception of the Church of England based on an experience of the local parish, not one single person made any reference to their bishop or diocese, good or bad. This was true for Anglicans as much as for non-churchgoers.

Yet the Church of England is structured around dioceses as much as parishes, around episcopal ministry as much as priestly. Does it matter if people do not know what a diocese is, or who their bishop is? Perhaps not. But if we imagine that ordinary people have much sense of these things or of identification with them, then we are mistaken.

Implications for the Mission of the Church

This is one of the most encouraging but also most challenging findings of all. It is simultaneously the easiest and hardest to address. A local church which engages positively and creatively with its community in very simple ways, offering a friendly welcome and professional service, can gain a good reputation not only for itself but to some extent for the whole Church of England. At the same time, a local church which is unwelcoming, unhelpful or unprofessional will develop a poor reputation which is hard to shake, and which also impacts on how local people see the church as a whole. And a church organized on the model of the Church of England will always find it very hard to ensure consistency in every parish. Being Church of England is not and cannot be a guarantee of quality.

For the Local Church

Every church should seek regular feedback from a wide range of local people, and especially from non-churchgoers who have had contact through life events (weddings, funerals, christenings). Give the option of anonymity. Consult those who made an enquiry and did not follow through as well as those who did. This may feel quite consumerist, but it will give a valuable perspective on the service we offer and enable us to improve, as well as communicating value to those whom we consult. Ask questions such as:

- How easy was it to make contact?
- How welcoming were we?
- How responsive were we to your needs?

- Would you recommend us to others?

Every church should seek feedback from external stakeholders. Local councillors are often a fount of knowledge on their patch. How do they think this church is seen locally? How could the church be a better partner to them?

Churches who are considering running community service programmes—such as food banks or work with homeless people—should be aware that, while the primary motivation is Christian mission, they are likely to receive a reputational boost from such activity.

Local churches could get better at telling the stories of what they are doing. Local media is often willing to cover church activity if it is interesting and if someone tells them about it. Consider appointing a local media liaison person from within the congregation.

Look at your signage through the eyes of a non-churchgoer. Would they understand it? What would it say to them? I would suggest the only message worth trying to get across on a notice board is, 'You are welcome here.'

Similarly, look at your website if you have one. Almost everyone is checking you out online before they visit. I am consistently amazed at how many churches do not keep their website up to date (it is late March as I write, and yesterday I looked at a church website that still had Christmas services all over it). Others are over-complex. Put the most important information on the home page. Think about the visuals as well as the words you use. What people want to know is:

- When are the services?
- Are there people like me there?
- Will I be welcome?
- Who is the vicar?

Check your information on A Church Near You. Is it current?

Consider advertising. When I was vicar of Ascension Balham Hill we bought advertising space on the escalators at Clapham South tube station. We made a video about the church and distributed it to every home in the parish.

For the National Church

How do we make more use of our key public figures, including the Archbishop of Canterbury, and other gifted communicators—not all of them bishops—who between them reflect the diversity of the church?

Is the present balance of responsibility and function between parish, diocese and National Church Institutions right?

How can we gain greater consistency across the church, so that we can have confidence in the welcome and service that people will receive from their local parish, considering selection, training, use of Ministerial Development Reviews, archdeacons' visitations and so on?

Key Factor 4: Embarrassed about God

5

God is the Interesting Thing

Evelyn Underhill wrote to the then-Archbishop of Canterbury, Cosmo Lang, in 1930, 'God is the interesting thing about religion, and people are hungry for God.'[8]

Most church leaders would, I hope, agree. Whatever else the church may do or stand for, at its core it is an institution that is about God, and for God.

Yet, in my research it was frequently commented that the church seems very embarrassed to talk about God. At an episcopal or national level, some feel that bishops are more confident talking about social issues than matters of doctrine or theology. At a local level, others note that those who run, for example, the food bank do not seem very interested or confident in articulating a Christian motivation for doing it, or using the contacts such ministry opens up for evangelism.

Use Words if Necessary?

St Francis of Assisi is sometimes (mis-)quoted as having said, 'Preach the gospel. Use words if necessary.' It seems that we have taken this flawed advice so much to heart that we do not use words even when it *is* necessary. Many Anglicans have a touching confidence that the care for their community which they express in social action—food banks, toddlers' groups and the like—communicate the gospel *in and of themselves* regardless of any verbalized Christian message which might be offered. This has almost certainly never been true at any point in the Church of England's history. It is certainly not true now, when people know less about the content of the Christian story than ever before.

In my round tables, some commented with all seriousness that they do not know what the church believes about God. One participant wondered aloud if we have stopped really believing in God and have decided to prioritize good works instead. When people stop to think about the Church of England at all, it is the local manifestations of community service or the national expressions of establishment Christianity which come to mind, not the gospel of Jesus Christ or an invitation to faith in and relationship with God.

One result of this is that people who are interested in exploring spirituality often do not consider the Church of England as a possible partner in that exploration. We are simply not associated with spiritual experience at all.

This relates to an argument which Tom Holland makes in his book *Dominion*, and which he also made in one of the round tables.[9] He argues that the values which we take as self-evident in twenty-first century Western culture—human rights and the worth of every individual, for example—are not universal values but are the product of the very thorough inculturation of Christian thought in the development of the West. The problem now is that when bishops or theologians talk about these things, they are no longer distinctive but sound like everyone else, so widely shared are these values. This leaves the church with the choice to either blend in, and so become irrelevant and invisible, or to speak about those things the church uniquely believes (what Tom calls 'all the weird, odd stuff').

Holistic Mission

In 2009 I undertook some doctoral research which was published under the title 'The Impact of Community Ministry on the Anglican Churches of South London.'[10]

I noted, 'A movement has emerged within the British church to live out a broader definition of the mission of God in the world expressing mission in community ministry and service as well as other forms of evangelism,' in contrast to a period earlier in the twentieth century when many churches saw community ministry as a distraction from the core task of the church: proclaiming the gospel of Jesus and inviting people to faith. Now, in many parts of the Church of England the pendulum has moved again, to a point where we are expecting community ministry and service to do all the evangelistic heavy lifting, and leaving non-Christian people at sea when they want to know what we believe or why we do what we do. (There are, of course, many wonderful instances where this is not the case, *Alpha* being an obvious one.) My research indicates that growing, healthy churches are likely to be ones where there is *both* a commitment to community service and practical action *and* a delight in communicating the Christian gospel and enabling people to make a response of some kind.

It is easy to assume that people know why we do what we do, but the evidence suggests this is not necessarily the case. In a culture with high levels of ignorance about Christianity, our motivation to engage in good works is not understood. Many members are not confident in verbalizing their faith. People do not associate the Church of England with a quest for spiritual experience. Our silence is read as implying that the church is embarrassed about God.

We do not need an either/or choice between community ministry and evangelism. Nor, in fact, do we need both-and. What we need is a recognition that all this belongs together and is in totality the manifestation of the kingdom of God in the world. The poor are fed, the sick are healed, the bound are set free and the good news of the death and resurrection of Jesus is preached to all. The movement back and forth from the church's declared confidence in God and the expression of that confidence in loving service should be intuitive and natural.

Implications for the Mission of the Church

Equip the Whole People of God as Witnesses

Not all are called to be evangelists, but every Christian is called to be a witness to what they have experienced of God in their own lives. In fact, I would argue that every Christian *is* a witness, whether they want to be one or not. The question is whether we will be good or bad witnesses. Every local church should run a regular programme to equip everyone to be good witnesses. (Full disclosure: my programme to address this, *Everyday Witness*, should be available by the end of 2021.)

Equip Church Leaders to Lead Evangelistically Fruitful Churches

Some church leaders, ordained and lay, are gifted evangelists, many are not. But every church needs to be a place where evangelistic fruit can grow. Regardless of tradition, every would-be ordained or licensed leader should have experience of fruitful evangelism. Every theological education institution and diocesan vocations team should ensure that training equips clergy for evangelism. Every church leadership team should talk and pray about evangelism together, building an evangelistic culture in the local church and offering opportunities for people to find faith. (And again, we have a programme coming called *Leading in Evangelism* to address this need.)

Engage in Public Theology and Cultural Witness

At a national level, the church needs to be able to engage in public discourse in a way which is culturally relevant and resonant, theologically rich, confident yet humble. There is work to be done on cultural witness, looking for overlaps between the longings of our culture as expressed through, for example, the arts, and the Christian story, and Bishop Graham Tomlin is doing some thinking around this. In a post-pandemic world, we need leaders who are able to articulate a vision of a better society couched in terms which specifically link back to our faith tradition and invite others to explore it with us, as many of our senior figures seek to do. We need to seek to shape the debate, not just respond to it.

6 Conclusion

I offer ten trends and ten questions drawn from the research that the church should pay attention to over the next decade.

10 Key Trends for the Future and Their Implications

- We anticipate that the decline in nominal Anglicanism will continue, meaning that new relationships and positive perceptions beyond the church will have to be created and nurtured.
- We anticipate that the focus on issues of racial justice and the celebration of LGBT+ people will continue to be mainstream, with consequent negative perceptions of the church if it is seen to be slow to respond.
- We anticipate that the trends towards online as a place to shop, socialize and access news, information, culture and entertainment, will continue. The mission opportunities of online church will continue as well. An increasing proportion of the worshipping community will gather online, either instead of or as well as offline, posing challenges for our practice around discipleship and sacraments, not to mention giving and finance.
- We anticipate that the position of the church at the centre of the establishment will be under continued scrutiny. A key moment for this will be the coronation of the next sovereign. The church will have to consider what case, if any, it wishes to make for this unique position in a multi-faith society. It is likely that governments of both main parties will be increasingly secular with diminishing understanding and appreciation of what the church brings to the table.
- We anticipate that we will continue to become a society divided around issues of power, wealth, opportunity and ideology, as demonstrated most recently by the Brexit debate and the unequal impact of COVID-19. Since many express the desire for institutions which can unite, and the belief that the church is equipped to play that role, we will have to consider how we can do that, and how that is held with our prophetic role to challenge and to speak up

for those without access to power. Is it possible to be the church for everyone and the church for the poor at the same time?

- We anticipate that social need in our society will continue to increase. Whatever the government's immediate plans to get the economy going again, national debts eventually have to be repaid, and historically this disproportionately impacts the poorest. Local authorities and charities are looking at frightening financial scenarios. The opportunities for us to engage in social action are likely to increase and to further outstrip our capacity to respond.

- We anticipate that, in the medium term, there will be a national debate about what kind of country we want to be post-COVID-19. Polls indicate that few people want to go back to the way things were. Some politicians are beginning to talk about 'building back better.' There is an opportunity to help shape this discussion, which is unlikely to come again.

- We anticipate an increasing interest in matters of faith and spirituality amongst the young. People now in their 20s may well be the third generation unchurched in their family. They are not so much post-Christian but pre-Christian, with little personal experience of the Christian church, interested in questions of belief and values, but with little interest in religious institutions. The church that seeks to engage them will have to speak of God, of spiritual encounter, of the values of the kingdom. This age group will not be drawn to a church that is seen to make few demands on them but may be attracted by a call to a life of radical discipleship.

- We anticipate that the world of work will change dramatically post-COVID-19, with increased home working and flexible working hours. This may mean that the church which wants to engage needs to move to a 24-7 model rather than a Sundays-plus-evenings model, which does not suit the moments that people are actually available. Online is important here. As people spend more time in their neighbourhood, there may be a greater desire to connect with local church rather than gathered, city-centre church, with particular opportunities for churches who are seen to be an asset to the local community.

- We anticipate that the focus on wholeness, healing and well-being which is already evident in our culture will be still more important in the future. There will be opportunities for the church to engage with this if we are able to articulate and demonstrate the gospel in ways which resonate.

- What do we want to say about God and how can we say it? How do we root all our actions explicitly in our theology? How do we 'motivate the million' so that our people are able to give confident witness to the faith they share and the work of God in their own lives?
- How do we navigate the tensions around the church's role in the public square, *eg* focusing on areas where we share common values with wider society and risking becoming invisible, as against emphasizing our distinctives and so perhaps becoming incomprehensible or controversial? Or the tension between the church's role at the centre of the establishment and our position on the edge with the marginalized and poor?
- How do we decide what social issues the church will engage with? How do we back up our words with action? What level of risk or controversy are we prepared to accept in developing a confident voice in the public square?
- Who specifically will speak on our behalf? How do we identify and resource those who have strengths to speak about God and about mission in the public square? How do we commission gifted communicators to be able to do more of this?
- What are the implications for the church of the collapse of nominal Anglicanism, and how do we work in a mission context where the majority no longer feel any connection to us? How do we develop our online presence and work confidently in the new mixed ecology? How can we embrace the online opportunities for evangelism?
- How do we balance and integrate our efforts around growing congregations with our commitment to social mission? As Liverpool's diocesan strapline puts it, 'More people knowing Jesus, more justice in the world.'
- With the increased profile of the national church during lockdown, is there a new role that the national church needs to play, and what would the implications of that be for dioceses? What role does the diocese have in the future? How do we link up a process of culture change across the church at national, diocesan and local church level? How do we accelerate that change while remaining a source of continuity and stability?

- How do we maintain our role as the Church for England when our leadership is not more diverse (class and education as well as gender and ethnicity)? How will we look like those we are called to serve? What actions will we take in pursuit of racial justice, and to ensure the church is safe for all?
- How do we ensure that the church is equally available for all people everywhere, recognizing the disparities in investment between parts of the country and types of area? How do we address the financial disparities between dioceses, which usually have nothing to do with missional strength and financial management, and everything to do with history and inherited reserves?
- How do we make appropriate demands on our people, welcoming all people at any stage of their faith journey, but then enabling them and challenging them to grow as missionary disciples of Jesus in the world?

I believe this research brings for the church important messages of *confidence* and *courage.*

We can have *confidence,* first, because the church continues to be positively regarded by many, albeit less so by some groups than others. Our culture may have drifted from Christian moorings but a residual fondness for the Church of England remains, together with a belief that it is uniquely placed to play a unifying role in society. More importantly, we need to recover our confidence in God and in the gospel, seeking to communicate that gospel before all else with humility and sensitivity, but also boldness.

This requires *courage,* which leads to the second point. We need courage to use our opportunities to speak of Jesus, particularly with younger spiritual seekers who do not think of us as an ally in that search. We need courage to listen to what God is saying to us through the situation in which we find ourselves. We need courage to change, letting go of good things from the past to become the church we are called to be for the future.

Appendix

Media Review

Primary sources were monthly media evaluation reports produced by the communications team at Church House. The period covered was March 2019 to May 2020. Over this period, I identified nine key themes of the Church of England's media coverage:

1. The Church of England as a force for unity
2. The Church of England being responsive to change
3. Safeguarding failures and cover-ups
4. LGBTQ+ issues and perceived homophobia
5. The Church of England as a force for justice
6. Churches, cathedrals, buildings and heritage
7. Decline in the church's numbers and reach
8. Local stories
9. Bishops and archbishops

Sometimes church people feel that they get a hard time from media reporting. My analysis suggests that this is not so. Of nine themes, five receive broadly positive coverage, three are generally negative (3, 4, and 7), and one can go either way (8). Some 60% or more of media coverage was perceived as positive, 6% as negative, with the rest being neutral.

Not all media outlets cover the Church of England equally. The church received the majority of its coverage from more establishment outlets, including the BBC, *The Times*, *The Telegraph* and the *Daily Mail*. Coverage from March 2020 onwards focused largely on the Church of England's response to COVID-19. Most coverage was positive, with the church being portrayed as sensible and cautious, concerned with public health above its own interests, engaged with those in most need and innovative in its use of digital media. The Archbishop of Canterbury volunteering at St Thomas's Hospital was positively reported. There was criticism of the church during this period over the closure of church buildings to their clergy, some of it coming from clergy themselves.

It is noticeable that little media coverage deals directly with what we might think of as the core business of the church—prayer, worship, evangelism—nor what the church understands of the Christian gospel. There is a question about whether this is because the media is not interested in this, or whether the church does not speak about it. It is clear that if the church wants to be able to talk about these things in the public space, we will have to shape our engagement with the media very intentionally with that end in mind.

Research Review

Sources (many of which are in the public domain) included:

1 Britain Thinks, CofE Audience Research, 2018
2 British Social Attitudes survey, 2019
3 Savanta ComRes, CofE mapping survey, 2017
4 Savanta ComRes for National Churches Trust, survey on visiting churches, 2018
5 Savanta ComRes for Theos, Brexit and churches, 2018
6 Savanta ComRes for TearFund, COVID-19 and Prayer, 2020
7 9 Dot, Qualifying Connections research for CofE Life Events, 2018
8 9 Dot, Christening Matters research for CofE Life Events, 2013
9 Britain Thinks, CofE Renewal and Reform online survey, 2020
10 Britain Thinks, Omnibus Survey, 2019
11 Britain Thinks, Coronavirus Diaries, 2020
12 'Living with Difference: Community, Diversity and the Common Good,' Report of the Commission on Religion and Belief in British Life, published by the Woolf Institute, 2015
13 Mission Map, by Dave Male, using work by ONS and BSA survey.

Round Table Discussions

Five round tables were held via Zoom between 27 May and 12 June, lasting 60 minutes. Grouping participants thematically had to be abandoned due to availability, except that the final round table consisted entirely of people aged 25 and under. The same structure of questions was used, although there were differences in the areas that groups chose to focus on. Participants included a mix of people who identified as Anglican and others who did not, people with specific expertise or experience (academics, historians, broadcasters, politicians, writers) and 'ordinary' people, of varied gender, age and ethnicity, although with less diversity of educational, regional or class background.

Questions for Round-table Discussion

General Questions for Round-table Discussion

- How do you think the Church of England is perceived today?
- What trends have shaped this perception?
- What do you think the perceived strengths are of what the Church of England offers?
- What are its perceived weaknesses?

Historic

- Historically, the Church of England has been at the centre of our national life. Do you think that is still the case now? Why / why not?
- If not, where does it find itself in contemporary society?
- What are the implications of that shift for the church?

Difference

- Are there differences between perceptions of the Church of England in different social groups (for example, by region, age, ethnicity, class, education etc)?
- What differences do you observe?
- What are the implications of those differences for a church that thinks of itself as being for all people in every place?

Future

- Looking to the future, how do you see the Church of England's position in society changing?
- What could the church do in response to those changes?
- Does the church have power to shape or influence those changes in the future, and if so, how?

Notes

1 H Rich, 'Growing Good: Growth, Social Action and Discipleship in the Church of England,' 2020: https://www.theosthinktank.co.uk/research/2000/01/31/the-grace-project (accessed 4 August 2020).

2 J Paxman, 'The Church of England's fight to survive,' *Financial Times Magazine*, 6 September 2017.

3 J Major, Speech to the Conservative Group for Europe, 22 April 1993: https://www.oxfordreference.com/view/10.1093/acref/9780191826719.001.0001/q-oro-ed4-00007018 (accessed 4 August 2020).

4 H Rich, *op cit.*

5 Savanta ComRes, 'Tearfund COVID-19 Prayer Public Omnibus Research,' April 2020: https://comresglobal.com/polls/tearfund-covid-19-prayer-public-omnibus-research/ (accessed 4 August 2020).

6 J Welby, *Reimagining Britain: Foundations for Hope* (London: Bloomsbury, 2018) and S Cottrell, *Dear England: Finding Hope, Taking Heart and Changing the World* (London: Hodder and Stoughton, 2021).

7 J Mitchell, *Big Yellow Taxi*, Reprise Records, 1970.

8 E Underhill, 'A letter from Evelyn Underhill to Archbishop Lang of Canterbury,' c 1930: www.anglicanlibrary.org/underhill/UnderhillLettertoArchbishopLangofCanterbury.pdf (accessed 4 August 2020).

9 T Holland, *Dominion: The Making of the Western Mind* (London: Abacus, 2020).

10 S Hance, 'The Impact of Community Ministry on Church Health in the Anglican Churches of South London,' 2009: https://place.asburyseminary.edu/cgi/viewcontent.cgi?article=1333&context=ecommonsatsdissertations (accessed 4 August 2020).